Tea
JUST FOR FUN
COLORING
BOOK

By: Sylvie Cyr

ARCHWAY
PUBLISHING

Archway Publishing books may be ordered through booksellers or by contacting:

Archway Publishing
1663 Liberty Drive
Bloomington, IN 47403
www.archwaypublishing.com
1 (888) 242-5904

ISBN: 978-1-4808-5284-6 (sc)
ISBN: 978-1-4808-5285-3 (e)

Print information available on the last page.

Archway Publishing rev. date: 02/16/2018

The Builder

The
Storekeeper

The Shopper

19

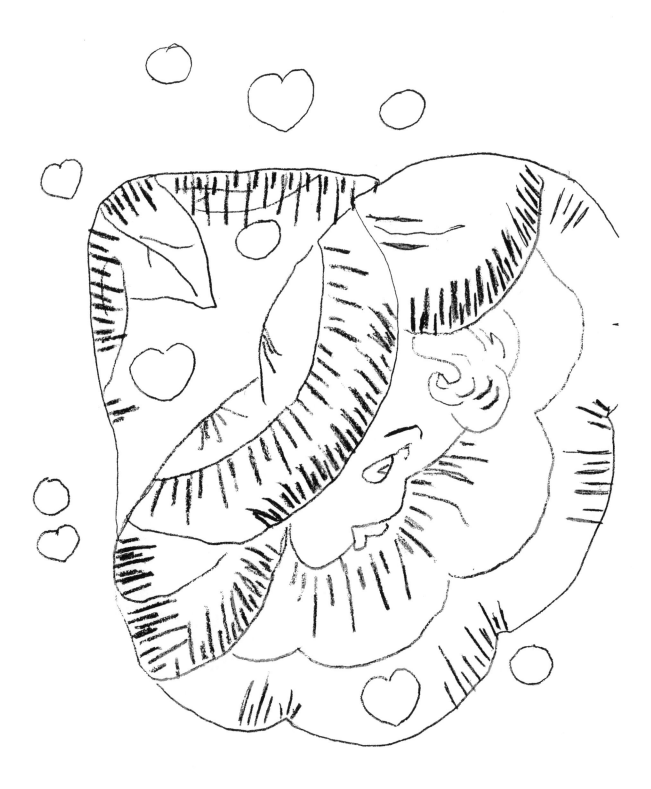

101

119

131

151

163

Printed in the United States
By Bookmasters